CRAFTS
OF MANY CULTURES
30 Authentic Craft Projects From Around The World

AURELIA GOMEZ

SCHOLASTIC
PROFESSIONAL**B**OOKS

New York • Toronto • London • Auckland • Sydney

Designed by Nancy Metcalf
Production by Intergraphics
Cover design by Vincent Ceci
Cover photo by John Parnell
Illustrations by Joe and Terri Chicko

ISBN 0-590-49182-2

. . . . . .

This book is
dedicated to the
indigenous peoples
of the earth.

_____

Mitakuye oyasin.

We are all related.

Somos mucho, somos uno.

_____

Contents

continued

Introduction

Crafts are a universal language of cultural expression. People in every culture make dolls, bags, rugs, vessels, textiles, and jewelry. The exact forms and particular characteristics are determined by geography, the materials available, and the personalities of the culture and of the artisan. Looking at and making craft objects give us an unparalleled opportunity to learn about each other and ourselves.

Children love craft projects, in which educators see evidence of many valuable learning experiences. When involved in hands-on art activities, children are actively solving problems, thinking critically, becoming visually literate, making aesthetic decisions, weighing and measuring, expressing themselves, using their imaginations, communicating with their peers, and developing motor skills.

Classrooms in the United States are filled with students from all over the world. The potential for intercultural exchange is unprecedented. I hope that these projects will enable you to begin a dialogue with your students about people in different parts of the world. Before you begin a project, find out if any of your students are familiar with the country or region you are focusing on. You may want to involve parents, relatives, and community members in some of your projects; the more connections, the better. Use your library to find books with pictures of crafts. Visit museums to see the real thing.

You may want to try out the projects before you present them to your students. But even if you are unable to do so, don't let that hold you back. Projects done with an attitude of experimentation usually yield wondrous results. Feel free to scale the activities up or down. Increase or decrease the level of sophistication of the projects. Use more or less elaborate materials. Some of the materials, like rice paper and armature wire, sound very exotic but are available in most craft and art supply stores. Above all, have fun.

I hope that these activities will encourage a rich exchange of ideas, abilities, and experiences among your students. As you and your children learn about specific cultural traditions from around the world, you will undoubtedly discover and develop the many talents that reside in your own classroom.

World Map

Northern Inspectorate

GREENLAND

Canada

NORTH AMERICA

United States of America

Southwest Native

Mexico

Guatemala

CENTRAL AMERICA

Panama

Ecuador

Peru

Atlantic Ocean

Haiti

Puerto Rico

CARIBBEAN

Brazil

SOUTH AMERICA

Poland

England **EUROPE**

Italy

Greece

Morocco

West Africa

AFRICA

Ghana

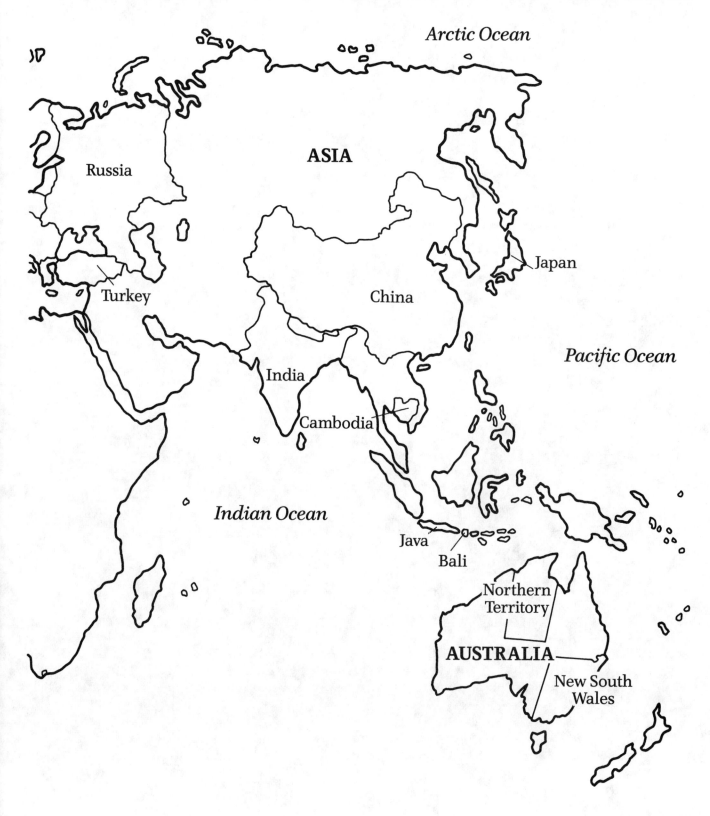

Arctic Ocean

ASIA

Russia

Turkey

Japan

China

India

Pacific Ocean

Cambodia

Indian Ocean

Java

Bali

Northern
Territory

AUSTRALIA

New South
Wales

NORTH AMERICA

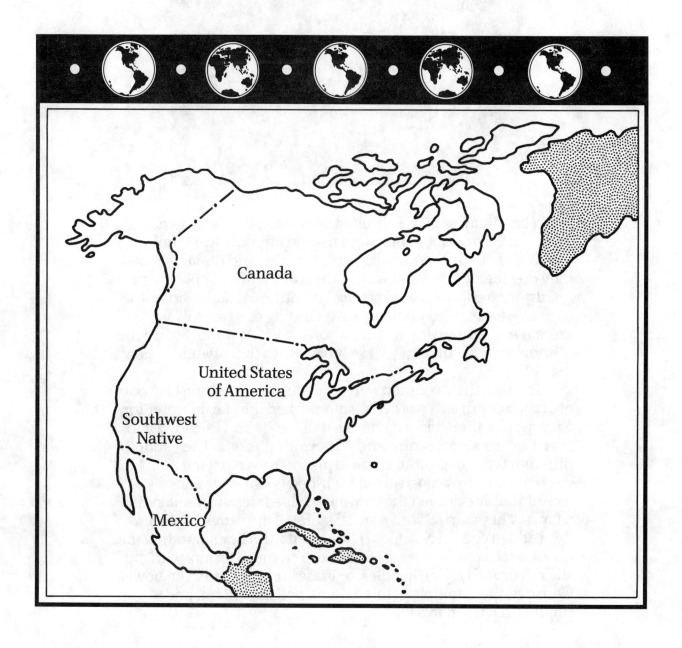

Canada

United States
of America

Southwest
Native

Mexico

Mimbres Pottery

The Mimbres people lived in southwestern New Mexico from A.D. 200 to 1200. They were named after the Rio Mimbres, the river that was their main source of water and possibly where they dug their clay. They painted the insides of their pots with highly ordered, often symmetrical paintings of daily activities such as weaving and planting and grinding corn as well as animal and human forms. Their bowls were so important to the Mimbres people that they were buried with their owners when they died.

To make their ceramic ware, the Mimbres first dug clay out of arroyos, or dried riverbeds. They soaked the clay in water for a few weeks, then formed it into small loaves and kneaded it to give it a consistent texture and remove air pockets. They added different types of ground stone to promote even drying.

The Mimbres constructed their bowls using the coil technique. They rolled the clay into coils—long, even, snakelike shapes. They started with a small spiral at the center of the base, then added coils of clay to form the contour. They smoothed the inside surfaces of the bowls and textured the exteriors with sticks, corncobs, pine needles, or grass bundles. After the bowls were dry, the Mimbres painted them, polished them, and finally fired them in a kiln.

You might discuss the origins of clay with your students. It comes from the earth. The Mimbres dug it it out of dried riverbeds, but you can also find clay by the banks of streams and rivers. It looks just like mud except that it is more pliable. If you can make it into a doughnut shape without its falling apart, it is clay. If not, it is mud.

HOW TO MAKE A
Mimbres Pot

Materials

- water
- pencils
- white and black tempera paint

- twigs
- brushes

- paper
- Clay ball, 2–3 inches in diameter, for each student

Directions

1. Roll clay into coils.

2. Turn one coil against itself to make a tight spiral. This is the bottom of the pot. Continue to add coils around the original spiral to make it larger.

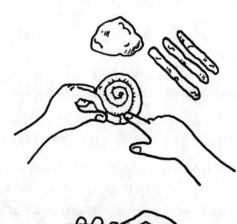

3. When the base fits comfortably in the palm of your hand, begin to add coils vertically, one on top of the other, to create the walls of the pot.

4. When all the coils are used up and you have the shape you like, it is time to smooth the inside of the pot. Cup the pot in one hand. Starting at the center of the base, push gently out and up with your thumb, smoothing and

until the entire interior has a consistent texture. Use a tiny amount of water to help you.

5. To texture the outside of the bowl, push the broken end of a small twig gently against the outside coils. Start at the top and continue going around the outside of the pot, covering the exterior with marks that give it a continuous, even texture. Set aside and let dry.

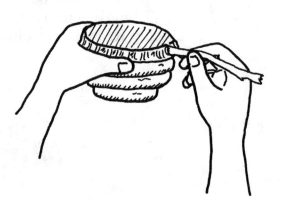

6. If you have access to a kiln, fire the pots. If not, use self-hardening clay. Before students paint their pots, you may want them to sketch their ideas. You can create an exercise in symmetry by giving them circular pieces of paper that have been folded in half. Students draw an animal, plant, or design form on one side and then draw or trace it on the other side, creating a balanced, symmetrical composition.

7. Coat pots with white tempera paint. Use just one or two layers, because more will chip off.

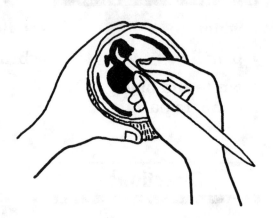

8. Sketch the design on the pot lightly with pencil.

9. Paint the design with black tempera paint.

Follow-up

- Set up a ceramic museum. Have students write descriptions of the decoration on their pot and display the pots and the descriptions in your classroom or school.

- Mimbres people made their own brushes from yucca leaves. They cut the leaves to the length they wanted and chewed the inner fiber to make soft bristles. Using natural materials from your area, have your students make brushes for painting.

- Read *When Clay Sings* by Byrd Baylor (Aladdin Books, 1972) with the class.

Carousel Animals

Modern carousels are operated by machinery and accompanied by recorded music; the animals are made out of metal, plastic, and fiber glass. Originally, carousels populated by wooden animals were turned by horses and oxen and accompanied by live music.

The name carousel is derived from the Italian *garosella* or the Spanish *carosella*; both mean "little war." In Europe, carousels were created to parallel equestrian games. In addition, riders could practice spearing rings with their lances.

Carousels arrived in the United States in the early 1800s. In 1850, Eliphalet S. Sculpture of Greenpoint, New York, registered a patent for the overhead suspension system that created a galloping effect. Though early American carousels had a huge array of animals—including dragons, rabbits, peacocks, camels, and elephants—they were frequently referred to as flying horse establishments. The various carousel animals were carved by wheelwrights, blacksmiths, unemployed ship mast carvers, and farmers. Carousel animal production was especially important in rural America, where carving the large animals was a good pastime for the long winter months.

HOW TO MAKE A
Carousel

Materials

- scissors
- tempera paint
- lazy susan

- glue
- brushes
- 5 tubes from paper towels

- masking tape
- fabric scraps, glitter
- 2 large pieces of corrugated cardboard

Directions

1. Cut 2 large circles (25–30 inches in diameter) out of corrugated cardboard for the top and bottom of the carousel.

2. Make several 1/2-inch vertical cuts in both ends of the paper towel tubes. Fold down the sections to make tabs.

3. Place 1 tube in the center of the bottom cardboard circle. Place the remaining 4 tubes around the perimeter of the circle.

4. Glue the tabs and attach them to the cardboard. Reinforce with masking tape. Let dry. Repeat to attach the top cardboard circle.

5. Paint the carousel with tempera paint and decorate it with fabric and glitter.

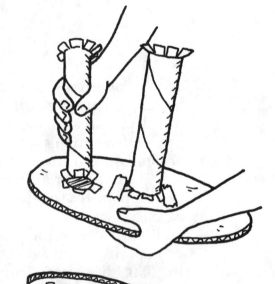

HOW TO MAKE
Carousel Animals

Materials

- pencils
- tape
- glue
- newspaper to cover tables

- scissors
- feathers, glitter
- 2 pipe cleaners
- drawing paper or newsprint

- markers
- paper scraps
- masking tape
- railroad board, cardboard, or tag board, $5\frac{1}{2} \times 7$ inches

Directions

1. Sketch ideas for carousel animals on drawing paper or newsprint.

2. Cut out the finished idea, tape it to the railroad board, and trace it.

3. Cut out the carousel animal.

4. Color the animal with markers and decorate it with different paper scraps, feathers, and glitter.

5. Take 2 pipe cleaners and twist them together. Place this "pole" vertically on the back side of the animal and attach it with masking tape.

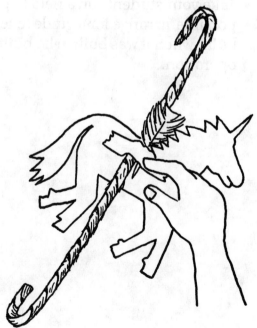

6. Fold each end of the pipe cleaner pole so that it fits inside the carousel. Position the pole and tape the ends to the top and bottom of the carousel. Cover the tape by gluing on decorative paper. Repeat to attach additional animals.

7. When the carousel is fully assembled, place it on top of the lazy Susan.

Follow-up

- Play carousel music and have students turn the carousel. Students may also enjoy improvising dance steps, imitating movements their animals might make, to the music.

- Invite students to write a story, dialogue, or poem from the point of view of a carousel animal. Each animal might identify its creator, what it is made out of, the favorite parts of its job, and its hopes and dreams.

- Carousels go round and round. With the class, brainstorm a list of other things that go round and round such as: wheels, records, and ferris wheels. How are they alike? How are they different?

- Take your students on a field trip to an antique carousel in your community. If possible, arrange for a guide to tell you the carousel's history including why it was built, when it was built, who built it, and how much it cost for a ride its first year in operation.

Papier-mâché Mermaids

The Spanish word for mermaid is *la sirena,* calling to mind the mythological sea nymphs whose singing lured sailors to destruction on the rocks surrounding their island. Many countries have stories about mermaids and sirens. They appear in Homer's *Odyssey.* Nineteenth-century English law claimed all mermaids found in coastal waters for the crown. There have been many sightings of mermaids by sailors: Columbus saw three, and Henry Hudson met one. In 1493, reports have it that a mermaid found at Edam was trained as a spinner, and in 1560 fishermen caught seven mermaids off the coast of Ceylon. As late as 1947, an 80-year-old fisherman saw a mermaid with a comb in its hand. Oceanographers would say these creatures were probably seals, dugongs, or manatees. But who knows for sure?

Mermaids are a traditional Mexican character. They appear holding guitars on painted tin, as earrings, whistles, and cloth dolls. This project is modeled after a contemporary Mexican mermaid sculpture from Oaxaca.

Papier-mâché is also a traditional craft of the Americas. *Papier-mâché* literally means "chewed-up paper" in French. In Mexico, papier-mâché is called *cartón piedra,* which translates as "stone cardboard." Pre-Columbian cartón piedra was made from amatl bark. This practical craft form has been used to make just about everything, including furniture and houses. When reinforced with wire, papier-mâché objects can last many years.

Since mermaids are a combination of human and fish forms, you may want to encourage your students to look at different types of fish forms, especially tails, before they begin drawing. You can also open this project up to encompass other mercreatures, such as merdogs, mercats, or merdeer.

HOW TO MAKE A
Papier-mâché Mermaid

Materials

- pencils
- newspaper
- yarn
- manila paper or cardboard

- drawing paper
- masking tape
- glue
- wheat or wallpaper paste

- scissors
- newspaper strips
- tempera paints

Directions

1. Sketch ideas for mermaids or mercreatures on paper. Cut out the creature and trace it onto manila paper or cardboard.

2. Cut the form out of the manila paper or cardboard.

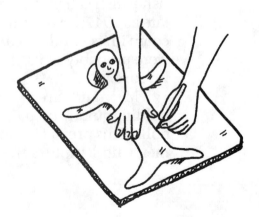

3. Crumple newspaper and tape it to the front and back of the form to add dimension. Encourage other ways of making shapes as well. Suggest that students look at sculptures, each other, objects, and fish to get an idea of the volume of different forms. Some students may want to work without the manila pattern.

4. Dip newspaper strips into paste, then wrap the strips around the taped form. Overlap the strips and apply several layers. Let dry.

5. Apply more papier-mâché if necessary. To make more elaborate forms, such as facial features, crumple newspaper into the desired shapes, place them on the form, and cover them with strips of paste-soaked newspaper.

6. When the mermaid is dry, paint it with tempera paint. Add hair by gluing yarn to the head.

Follow-up

- Hang the mermaids in your room to create a feeling of swimming underwater.

- Use the mermaids as a springboard for writing and storytelling. Here are some ideas for questions to ask. What is your mermaid's (or mercreature's) name? What does it eat? Who is in its family? Where does it live? What is its home like? What songs does it sing? Does it know any jokes?

Huichol Yarn Paintings

*T*he Huichol Indians are from Jalisco and Nayarit, states in
Mexico on the Pacific Coast. They are a Pre-Columbian people
who have retained their cultural identity by retelling their
stories and myths in paintings made of yarn, wood, and
beeswax. A Huichol painter covers plywood with beeswax, then
uses a screwdriver or sharp tool to scratch a design into it. The
board is set out in the sun. When the beeswax is soft enough, the
painter presses one or two strands of yarn at a time into the
design, and the picture emerges.

Huichol legends are about heroes and heroines and the
different powers of plants and animals. Traditionally, the
Huichol are farmers. Corn, their primary crop, figures in many
of their yarn paintings. Huichol children learn their stories
at a young age. When they are four and five, they begin to
draw them.

HOW TO MAKE A
Huichol Yarn Painting

Here are two different methods for making a Huichol yarn painting. The colored pencil version is for a wide range of levels. The yarn version is quite difficult. Manipulating yarn and glue can be very frustrating. However, it is more authentic and may be worthwhile to try with highly dexterous students. You can combine elements of both versions by having students add one or two pieces of yarn to their colored pencil versions.

Colored Pencil Version

Materials

- colored pencils
- paper, 4 × 4 inches

Directions

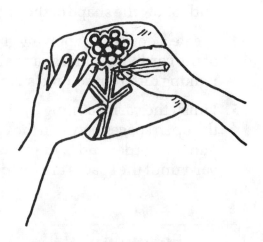

1. Draw the outline of a plant, animal, person, or other shape in the center of the square of paper.

2. Emphasize the outline by drawing a dark line, a bright line, or a very thick line around it.

3. Using different colored pencils, fill in the shape by drawing a series of lines that echo its curves and angles. (You can think of the colored pencil lead as yarn or string.)

4. Create a border by drawing different shapes and designs around the edges of the paper. Color in the space between the central shape and the border.

Yarn Version

Materials

- pencils
- brightly colored yarn (thicker yarn is easier to handle)
- cardboard squares, 4 × 4 inches
- scissors
- glue

Directions

1. Draw the outline of a plant, animal, person, or other shape in the center of the cardboard square.

2. Apply glue to the outline and press yarn into the glue, one or two strands at a time.

3. Spread glue inside the shape and press yarn into it. Use one or two strands of yarn at a time and follow the shape of the outline.

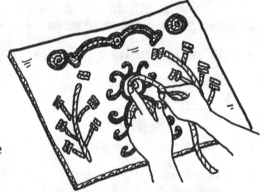

4. Create a border by applying glue to the edges of the cardboard. Press yarn along the edges, making different colored stripes.

5. Finish the yarn painting by spreading glue in the open spaces between the central shape and the border and laying down strands of yarn until the spaces are filled.

Follow-up

- Assemble the individual yarn paintings to form a class mural.
- Use the yarn paintings as a border for a wall map of Mexico.
- Invite students to write their own legends about heroes and heroines.

Eskimo Soapstone Carvings

Long Arctic nights and the isolated life of nomadic Canadian Eskimo families gave rise to a culture rich in myths and legends. Canadian Eskimo stories express the life of spirits, the hunt for animals, and the value of family cohesion. Having no tradition of flat or two-dimensional artwork in the European tradition, and no books or TV screens, Canadian Eskimos carved sculptures from walrus ivory, bone, antler, and stone. Their sculpture is characterized by innovation rather than derivation or traditionalism. For the Canadian Eskimo, art is the act of living in harmony with nature. There is no word for beauty in their language. The integrity of a carving—how well it is made—is their criteria for beauty.

The subjects of Canadian Eskimo carvings are people, animals—including fish, bears, caribou, owls, lemmings, sea pigeons, and musk oxen—and combinations of human and animal forms. The sculptures are imbued with the sense of life within the forms that reflect a hunting society's knowledge of anatomy and spirit. The figures are usually very graceful, smooth, and well polished.

The eastern and central Arctic portions of Canada have many rich deposits of semisoft carving stones, including soapstone. The stone is usually found along barren coasts, often below the tide line. Soapstone is quarried during the summer, then carved and polished during more inclement weather.

HOW TO MAKE AN
Eskimo Soapstone Carving

Materials

- **clay ball, 3–5 inches in diameter, for each student**
- **loop clay tools or paper clips bent into a loop shape**
- **water**

Directions

1. Drop the clay lightly onto a table, flattening several of the surfaces. The purpose is to make the piece of clay resemble a rock.

2. Look at your clay rock and visualize the form of a human, animal, or imaginary creature.

3. Use your clay tool to carve away the clay, revealing the form you imagined. Be sure to turn the clay while you work, enabling you to carve the form from all sides.

4. Dip your finger in water and smooth your clay carving.

5. Use the end of your clay tool to draw any details, features, or textures onto the figure. Let dry.

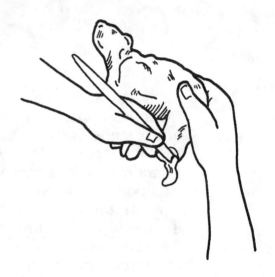

Follow-up

- Display the Eskimo soapstone carvings in your classroom. Pass out 3 × 5-inch cards to your students. Have them pick out someone else's carving and describe it as succinctly as possible, using fewer than 10 words. Add the cards to the display.

- Have your students write about the carvings as though they have come to life. They can describe the process of waking up, figuring out who they are, what happens when they move, and any adventures they may have.

- Read the following Canadian Eskimo song to your class.

Ayii Ayii

I walked on the ice of the sea,
And wandering I heard my song of the sea,
The great sighing of the new-formed ice.
Go then, strength of soul
Bring health to the place of feasting.

CENTRAL AMERICA

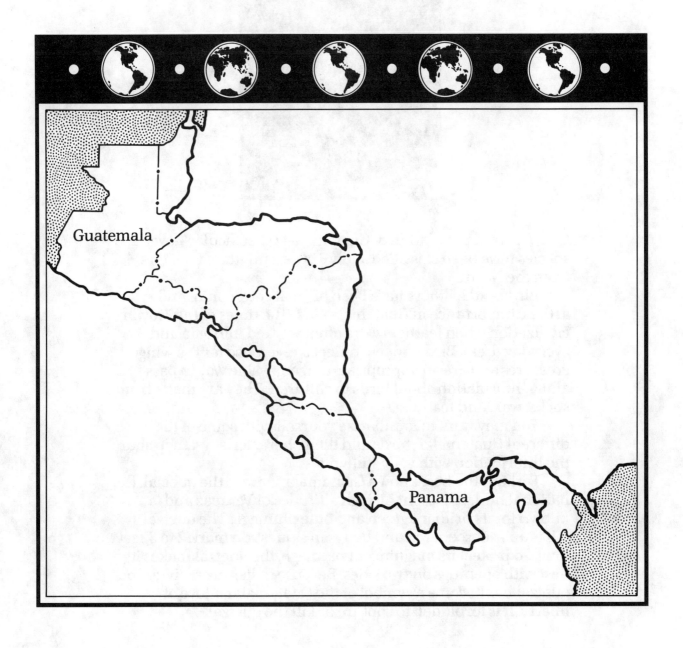

Guatemala

Panama

Bird Puppets

*T*he bird population of Guatemala is spectacular—over 900 species have been classified. Only 190 are migratory visitors from the North.

Birds and feathers have been of great ceremonial and artistic importance in Guatemala since the times of the Mayan civilization when feathers were often worked into gala and everyday dress. Bird puppets reflect a reverence for the winged creatures and are an appropriate and enjoyable way to pass along information about birds to children. They are made from sticks, wax, and feathers.

You may want to familiarize yourself with some of the different Guatemalan birds and their characteristics, then share the information with your students.

Perhaps the best-known Guatemalan bird is the quetzal, the national bird. It lives in the high altitudes of Verapaz and is known for its brilliant green and blue plumage. The quetzal's tail is an iridescent red and hangs in a question mark 2 to 3 feet long. To protect its magnificent plumage, the quetzal makes its nest with openings on two sides. Because it dies in captivity, the quetzal has become a symbol of the Guatemalans' love of liberty. It is forbidden to capture or kill the quetzal.

Other birds include the *cuchucito,* which has a call that sounds like a small dog's bark. Guatemalans believe that the bird's call forecasts earthquakes, war, death, and other major disasters. Of the many types of owls found in Guatemala, one is called *guía de león* or the lion's guide, because it flits from tree to tree emitting short, sharp notes when it sees a lion or puma on the prowl. The *cenzontle,* or "bird of 400 voices" (mockingbird), is sought after as a pet. It lives happily in captivity and is an inspiration for music. The *oropéndola,* the golden oriole, inhabits hot climates. It builds a long, hanging nest from the branches of dead trees. Some trees may have as many as 50 to 100 nests built closely together. *Oropéndolas* fly into the tree top and out the bottom in a steady stream. The *azacuán* is a type of falcon that migrates north in large numbers in April and May. It returns in late October, after the rains. Flying as far north as Canada and as far south as Argentina, the *azacuanes* are charged with opening and closing the springs for rain.

HOW TO MAKE A
Bird Puppet

Materials

- clay piece, 3–4 inches in diameter, for each student

- stick or dowel

- feathers (Collect them from outdoors, buy them at a craft store, or have your students make them out of paper.)

Directions

1. Form the clay into a real or imaginary bird shape by pressing, pinching, and molding it with your hands and fingers. Try to keep it all in one strong piece.

2. Insert the stick into the bird's body.

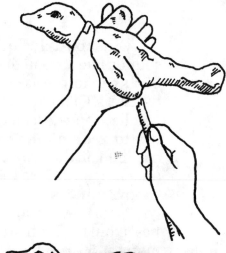

3. Insert feathers into the bird. Let dry.

Follow-up

- Have students make nests for the birds out of twigs and clay.
- Let your class take the bird puppets outside for a puppet parade.
- Have your students create a bird puppet play.
- Have students research real birds that are indigenous to Guatemala. Invite them to write short reports to share with their classmates.

Molas

*M*olas are brightly colored, intricately designed appliquéd fabric panels that are made by Cuna Indian women from the San Blas islands of Panama. Molas are a relatively new art form, having appeared in the last century. The word *mola* originally referred to an entire piece of clothing, a dress or blouse. Now *mola* signifies just the brightly colored panels that appear on the front and back of Cuna blouses.

Molas are an important part of the everyday costume of the Cuna women, who also wear wraparound sarongs, beaded bracelets, gold nose rings, and vertical stripes down the middle of their noses. Cuna men wear traditional Western attire.

Women make molas in their spare time, using machine-made cloth sewn by hand. Fabric is layered with two to seven layers of fabric, sewn together, cut, and then resewn to create an intricate, multicolored design. Children learning how to sew molas make two-layer molas, using their mother's scraps.

Older molas depict scenes from everyday life such as gathering coconuts or paddling canoes. Compositions also included indigenous plants and animals as well as completely abstract geometric designs. Contemporary molas often have numbers, letters, and trademarks incorporated into their designs. You may want to look at the abstract elements of labels and trademarks with your students. Then they can choose to use them in their mola design if they like.

HOW TO MAKE A
Mola

Materials

- scissors
- paper scraps

- pencils
- construction paper, at least two 9 × 6-inch pieces of contrasting colors for each student

- glue

Directions

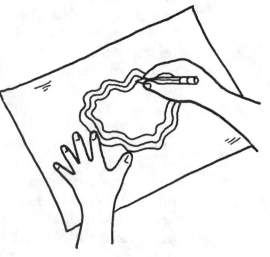

1. Draw a simple design using one continuous line on the first piece of construction paper. The line does not have to connect to itself. Use a plant, animal, person, logo, or abstract shape for your design.

2. Draw a second continuous line about 1/4 inch away from the original line.

3. Draw a third continuous line about 1/4 inch away from the original line on the other side. There should be 3 lines, with the original line in the center.

4. Cut along the outer line in order to remove the entire design from the piece of construction paper.

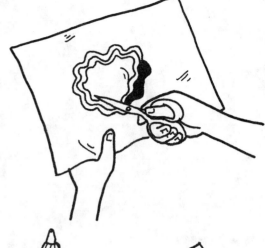

5. Glue the design to the contrasting piece of construction paper.

6. Cut leftover paper or additional scraps into shapes to glue to your design. Let dry.

Follow-up

- Put the molas together to make a large wall hanging to display in your classroom.

- Have students draw mazes, using molas for inspiration. Let pairs of students attempt to solve each other's mazes.

CARIBBEAN

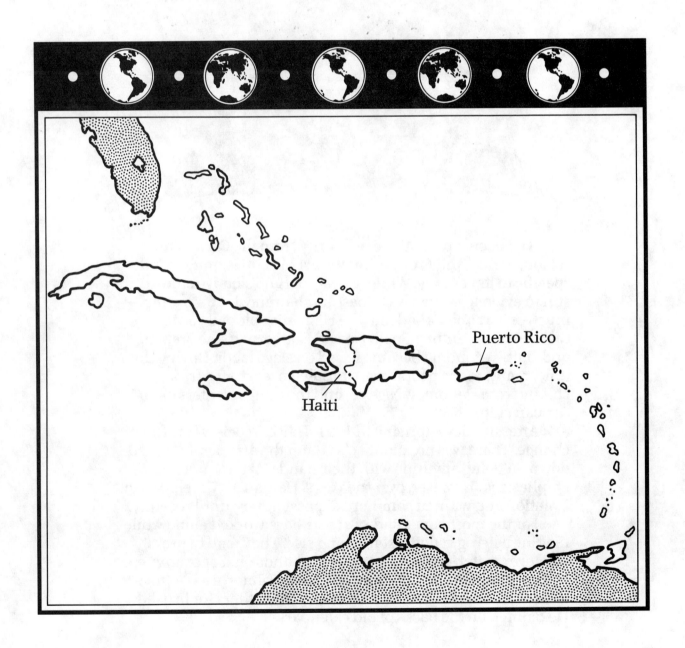

Puerto Rico

Haiti

Steel Drum Cutouts

The people of Haiti are primarily from the Caribbean region, Africa, and Europe, but the art of Haiti is unique and specific to its country. While aspects of Haiti's native culture are still in evidence—maize, canoes, and hammocks, for example— much of it was absorbed into the Hispanic colonial culture in the sixteenth century. Spain turned Haiti over to the French, and Haiti's economy became based on slave labor. During this time, many, many people were brought over from Africa, chiefly from Dahomey, Nigeria, and the Congo, centers of African culture.

After the slave uprising in 1791, Haitian society was full of change. There was no middle class, and the aristocrats looked down on doing anything with their hands. Art was not emphasized. However, over the years, Haitian art developed in isolation and without commercial possibilities, until recently.

For the most part, Haitian artists have worked alone while making a living at doing something else. They tend to use whatever materials they can get their hands on. For example, Hector Hyppolite, a well-known Haitian painter, used leftover household enamel for paint and chicken feathers for brushes. He painted on the backs of old calendars.

Steel drum cutouts are related to a long history of ironwork in Haiti that originated in Africa. Haitian blacksmiths flatten out empty steel oil drums. They draw a design, frequently choosing characters from their favorite stories, and chisel the shapes out of the steel. Then they hammer and forge the flat shapes into their final form. The finished sculptures are displayed on pedestals or shown lying flat.

HOW TO MAKE A
Steel Drum Cutout

Materials

- scrap paper
- glue
- black tempera paint
- pencils
- masking tape
- cardboard (preferably recycled from cereal boxes, tissue boxes, or boxes from other household products)
- scissors
- brushes or black crayons

Directions

1. Sketch an idea on scrap paper. Your drawing should be simple and have a strong outline.

2. Unfold and flatten cardboard boxes to create as many large, flat areas as possible.

3. Transfer your drawing onto the cardboard and cut it out. Also cut out a section of extra cardboard to use as a prop later. (An L shape cut from a box fold is helpful.)

4. Paint the cardboard cutout with black tempera paint, or color it with black crayon. Let dry.

5. Glue the cardboard onto the back of the cutout, positioning it so the cutout can stand independently. Tape to reinforce. Let dry.

Follow-up

- Set up displays of cutout sculptures in your classroom or school. Have each student write a descriptive label about his or her work on a card. Shuffle the cards and pass them out. Have students match the cutouts with the descriptions.

- Have students bring in materials from home that they don't need—fabric scraps, different types of plastic, cardboard, and so forth. Divide the class into groups and have them make sculptures using their discarded "treasures."

Gourd Bowls

Gourds are used in a variety of ways in the Caribbean. Once dried and hollowed, gourds can be transformed into containers, a variety of musical instruments, or cups for drinking chocolate. Small gourds, the size of a hen's egg, are made into tops for children.

In Puerto Rico, gourds are used to make bowls for serving and eating food. First the gourds are dried, then soaked in water so the outer skin can be peeled off. Then they are cut in half. Next, the seeds and pulp are removed and the exterior is polished with a rough herb. To decorate the gourds, a pattern is traced on the exterior with a pencil or sharp tool, then carved with a knife. The gourds are sometimes stained or burned to create exciting color combinations.

HOW TO MAKE A
Gourd Bowl

Materials

- balloons
- containers for paste and water
- scissors

- newspaper strips
- water
- pencils

- brushes
- wheat paste or wallpaper paste
- tempera paint

Note: Have students work in pairs for steps 1–3.

1. Blow up your balloon into a gourd-like shape.

2. Cover your balloon with papier-mâché by dunking strips of newspaper into the paste and laying them on the balloon. Overlap the newspaper strips. Cover the balloon with at least three layers of newspaper and paste. Let dry.

3. Look at the balloon shape and visualize how to divide it in half so you will get two symmetrical bowl shapes. With a pencil, draw a line around the balloon. Cut along the line with scissors, dividing the papier-mâché gourd in half.

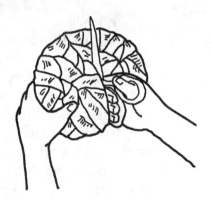

4. Paint the bowl, inside and out, with one or two colors of tempera paint. (Most gourd bowls range in color from tan to dark brown. You can choose to limit the palette to shades of brown or encourage less traditional color combinations.) Let dry.

5. Turn the bowl over, so the bottom is up. Draw a design motif, animals, or people on the outside with a pencil.

6. Using one or two colors of tempera paint, paint along the penciled lines. Let dry.

| **Follow-up** |

- Research the many ways gourd bowls were used. Then display the bowls with descriptions of how they were made and what they were used for.

- Invite children to give their gourd bowls as holiday presents. (Be sure to stress to children that the bowls should *not* be used for storing or serving food.)

SOUTH AMERICA

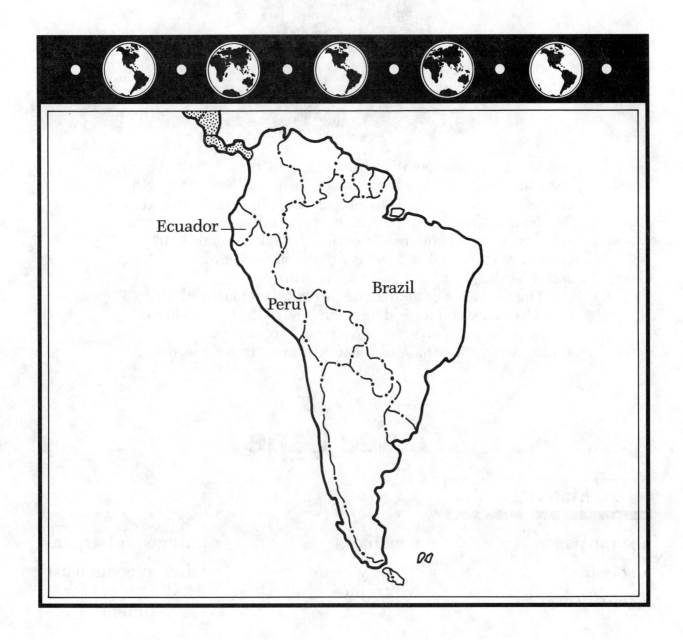

Ecuador

Peru

Brazil

Dance Capes

Every September in Sapallanga, Peru, there is a dance festival. The dances are of Indian, Spanish, and African origin, are performed by from 12 to 24 men. The dancers are called *Garibaldis,* after the nineteenth century Italian expatriate who aided Peru's independence from Spain. Each Garibaldi carries an anchor and a bell and wears a dance cape. They are accompanied by drums and a brass band.

The dance capes themselves are small, not larger than 3 × 3 feet. They have collars and flare out toward the bottom hem, but each has a slightly different shape. They are heavily embroidered with images of historic events from Peru's past.

HOW TO MAKE A
Dance Cape

Materials

- scrap paper
- scissors
- fabric scraps

- pencils
- fabric glue or white glue

- buttons and sequins
- fabric piece at least 24 × 36 inches for each student

Directions

1. Sketch ideas for special events to celebrate on scrap paper. You can draw pictures of things that really happened, or show imaginary events.

2. Spread out the fabric and imagine how your drawing will cover it.

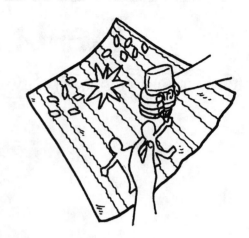

3. Draw the important shapes from your sketch onto fabric scraps and cut them out.

4. Arrange the fabric shapes on the larger fabric piece. Glue them in place. Let dry.

5. Glue buttons and sequins to the cape designs. Let dry.

6. To wear the cape, simply tie the top 2 corners around your neck.

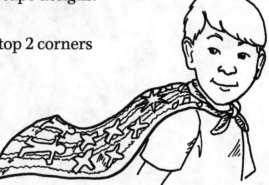

Follow-up

- With the class, listen to "Land of the Incas," a tape of Peruvian music. Help students identify the instruments. A good source for this tape as well as other multicultural and multilingual materials is Claudia's Caravan, P.O. Box 1582, Alameda, CA 94501, (510) 521-7871.

- Have students share their capes by wearing them in front of the class and taking turns describing the scene on the back.

- Have a parade in which your students wear their dance capes.

Fiesta Headdresses

*I*n mountainous areas of Ecuador, in the provinces of Cotopaxi and Tungurahua, people hold a winter fiesta every year with special costumes and dances in preparation for planting. The men dance in the streets and plazas to drummed rhythms and melodies from flutes called *pinguyo* and panpipes called *rondador.* They wear painted hats, frequently bowlers, with coins suspended around the brim. It is an honor to be one of the *danzante,* who rent their costumes from the families who own them.

The fiesta headdresses sit on top of the hats, covering the curved crown and resting on the brim. They are made of fabric with a collage of buttons, charms, and ribbons that symbolize wealth. Feathers and ribbons stream down the back, making a *cola,* or tail. In addition to the fiesta headdresses, the dancers wear masks and costumes embroidered with foil, braid, and ribbon.

HOW TO MAKE A
Fiesta Headdress

Materials

- scissors
- stapler
- feathers, buttons, fabric scraps, rick rack, sequins, glitter

- glue
- ribbon

- crayons or craypas
- brown paper (from recycled grocery bags)

Directions

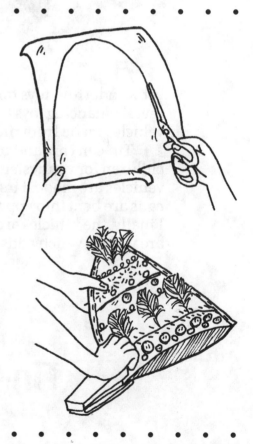

1. Cut 2 inverted U shapes out of brown paper for each student. These form the front and back of the headdress. Make sure that both pieces are wide enough so that when the bottoms are stapled together they will fit over your students' heads.

2. Draw designs on the paper with crayons or craypas. Experiment with different types of lines: straight, squiggly, zigzags, dotted, thick, thin, and so forth.

3. Decorate by gluing on feathers, buttons, fabric scraps, rick rack, sequins, and glitter. Let dry.

4. Staple the 2 shapes together at the bottom.

5. Staple on ribbons.

Follow-up

- Have your students wear their fiesta headdresses in a parade around your school.

- Invite students to wear their fiesta headdresses during music and movement time.

Tin-can Vehicles

At Brazilian markets, it is very common to find simple—yet wonderful—toys for children. Rag dolls, wooden trucks, and metal balancing toys are available as well as a variety of small vehicles made from tin cans.

Tin-can cars and trucks are made by adults and older children for youngsters and the marketplace. Here is how the vehicles are made: First, several cans are washed out. Next, the cans are bent into appropriate shapes, then nailed together. Finally, the vehicles are painted. Sometimes the colorful labels are visible, which adds to the charm of these durable toys.

HOW TO MAKE A
Tin-can Vehicle

Note: In the interest of safety, cardboard boxes will be used instead of tin cans. You might want to point out to students that both craft projects represent creative ways to recycle.

Materials

- glue
- small to medium-sized cardboard boxes (cereal boxes, shoe boxes

- scissors
- scraps of cardboard
- tempera paint

- pencils
- newspapers (to cover tables while working)

Directions

1. Arrange several boxes to create a car or truck shape. Use a pencil to indicate where the doors, windows, wheel wells, etc., will go.

2. Use scissors to cut out pencil-marked doors, windows, wheel wells, etc.

3. Glue the boxes together.

4. From scraps of cardboard and other boxes, cut out additional shapes for wheels, passengers, cargo, etc.

5. Glue those shapes to the vehicle.

6. Paint with tempera paint. Let dry.

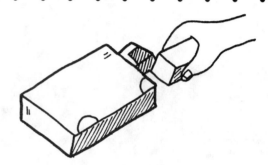

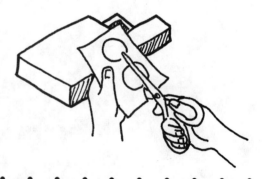

Follow-up

- Use the vehicles as a springboard to writing. Here are a few ideas:

  1. Pretend your toy vehicle is real. Where do you want to go? Describe your dream trip.

  2. Pretend your toy vehicle is real. Create a list of all the ways you can use it to help your community.

  3. Imagine that someone else wants to make a vehicle just like yours. As clearly as you can, write down every step it took to make it.

AFRICA

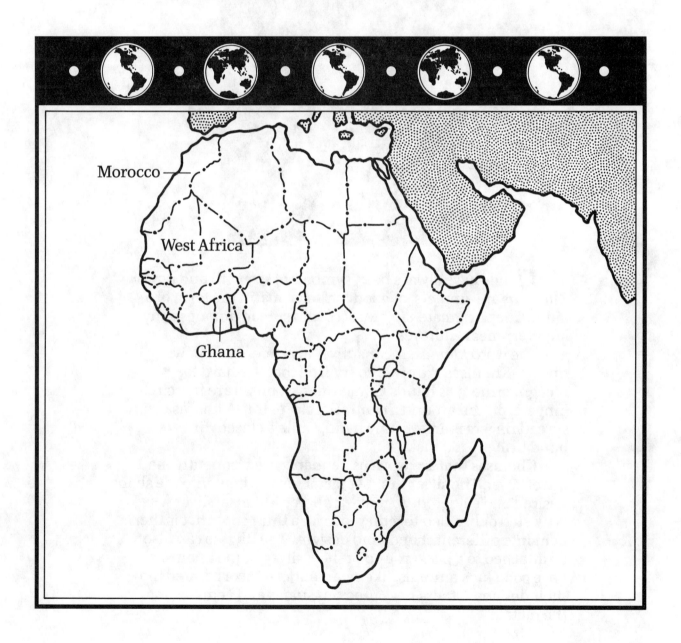

Khamsas (Good Luck Hands)

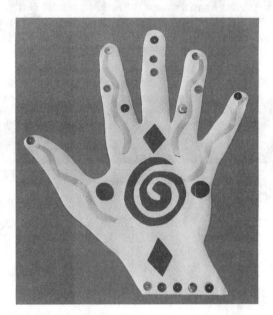

Hands have always been symbols of strength and power. *Khamsas* are amulets, or good luck charms, in the form of a hand. They originated in Morocco and spread among many Mediterranean cultures.

The word *khamsa* means "five" and refers to the five fingers. Khamsas are often so stylized that it is hard to recognize them as hands. Sometimes khamsas are five circles (fingers) placed around a central circle (palm). A khamsa with spread fingers is an averting hand, while a closed, fingered hand brings good luck.

Khamsas that are worn as pendants are frequently made out of silver. The silver in sheet metal form is bent into the shape desired and soldered. To make a filigree khamsa, silver wire is twisted or braided together to form a thick rope that is then bent into different shapes and designs. The filigree can also be attached to a background of sheet silver. Some khamsas have good luck animals, like salamanders, incorporated into their designs. Others have precious stones and gems set into the metal.

HOW TO MAKE A
Khamsa

Materials

- pencils
- sequins
- scissors
- 2 pieces of metallic foil paper or regular construction paper, 6½ × 10 inches, in different colors, for each student
- glue

Directions

1. Place your hand on the first piece of paper, making sure it fits within the edges. Position fingers in a way that pleases you.

2. Trace around your fingers, hand, and wrist.

3. Cut out the shape of your hand. Save the scraps.

4. Draw shapes and designs on the second piece of paper that will fit within the hand shape.

5. Cut out the shapes and glue them onto the khamsa.

6. Add more shapes of the contrasting color, or build on top of the shapes with scraps of the original color.

7. Glue on sequins. Let dry.

Follow-up

- Mount khamsas on cardboard or construction paper and display by hanging them around your classroom doorway.

- Have students write good luck wish poems, stories, or notes.

- Students can make mini-khamsas out of construction paper and wear them on string necklaces.

Adire (Tie-dye)

*A*mong the many ways to tie-dye, the simplest method is to take cotton fabric, tie it in knots, and immerse it in dye. You can also use rubber bands or string to bind sections of fabric before dyeing it. Gathering fabric around small objects—pebbles, beans, corks, marbles, or beads, for example—and then binding it with string will create yet another effect.

Today, the art of tie-dye is flourishing in the West African countries of Nigeria, Ghana, Liberia, Ivory Coast, Sierra Leone, Benin, and Cameroon. The Yoruba, a West African people, call the fabric *adire*. They sew elaborate patterns with raffia, then pull the raffia very tight, gathering and puckering the fabric. Then they place the bundles of wrinkled fabric in pits filled with indigo or aniline dye. After dyeing, the fabric is rinsed unstitched, and dried. Instead of ironing the cloth, the Yoruba pound it with wooden mallets and sprinkle it with indigo to create a shiny surface.

Adire

Materials

- scissors
- needles
- rubber bands
- buckets

- muslin or cotton sheeting
- raffia or thread
- blue fabric dye

- pencils
- buttons
- water

Directions

1. For each student, cut 1 rectangular section of fabric that is large enough to cover his or her chest and back.

2. Fold the fabric in half, and cut an opening for the neck and head. (A T shape works nicely.)

3. Using a pencil, draw a few simple lines across the fabric. You may want to talk about different types of lines and have your students identify straight, wavy, curly, and zigzag lines.

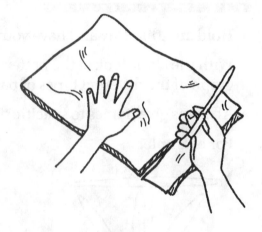

4. Thread a needle with raffia or thread and tie a button securely at the end.

5. Using a running stitch, sew over the lines you have drawn. When you come to the end of a line, tie the end of the raffia securely to another button. Make sure the button is *not* sewn to the fabric.

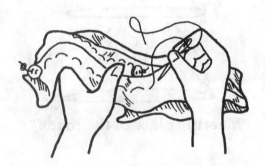

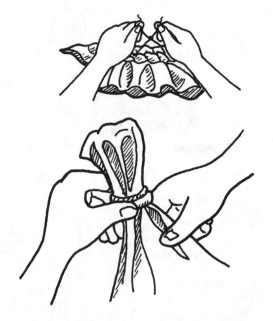

6. When you have sewn over all the lines, gather the fabric by pulling the buttons toward each other. Tie the raffia together tightly.

7. Gather the remaining sections of fabric and bind them with rubber bands.

8. Immerse the fabric in buckets filled with dye. Follow the instructions, and do not let children handle the dye.

9. Rinse the fabric and let dry.

10. Cut the raffia carefully and undo the rubber bands.

11. Iron the tie-dye creations.

Follow-up

- Hold an Adire Day and have your students wear their creations.

- With the class, look at the patterns on the clothing your students wear. Make a graph of the different types of patterns: stripes, polka dots, plaids, and so forth.

- Africans give names to specific tie-dye patterns.

   For example:

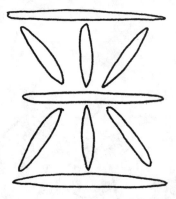

"Meeting place of the roads"

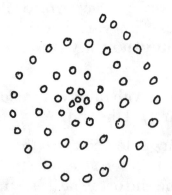

"Welcome to the masquerade"

Have your students draw their own patterns and name them.

Linguist Staffs

*L*inguist staffs are tall wooden sticks that African leaders use as an emblem of their position. They derive from the European tradition of cane holding and were originally referred to as messenger sticks. As a means of deferring to his authority, someone in Ghana first carried a European cane when speaking to a chief. Eventually, this use of the cane became associated with the role of the linguist, or spokesperson, and spread beyond Ghana.

The staffs themselves are carved out of wood and covered with gold leaf. The Ghanians embellished the traditional staffs by topping them with sculptural decorations that represented proverbial messages. These messages were intended to remind the staff holders of basic values and morals and thus prevent power from going to their heads. For example, a sculpture that depicted a king holding an egg meant that the king must take care of his people. A representation of a bush cow and an elephant referred to a traditional proverb: "The bush cow says that if the elephant is not around, the bush cow is the mountain." In other words, when a more important person is absent, the lesser person thinks of himself or herself as great.

You may want to share with your students these additional African symbols and the sayings associated with them.

Scorpion: "The scorpion exists in thunder." (Persevere in the face of difficulty.)

Key: "If I lock it, nobody can open it." (A message from parents to children meaning the parent has the final say.)

Chameleon: "The world is a chameleon's skin." (A warning to someone of great wealth who thinks he or she will never lose it.)

HOW TO MAKE A
Linguist Staff

Materials

- sticks, dowels, or broom handles
- brushes

- clay ball, 3–4 inches in diameter, for each student

- yellow or gold tempera or acrylic paint

Directions

1. Insert one end of the stick into the ball of clay, and press the clay around the stick.

2. Form the clay into a shape or figure that would be a good reminder or inspiration for a leader. Let dry.

3. Paint the staff with yellow or gold paint. Let dry.

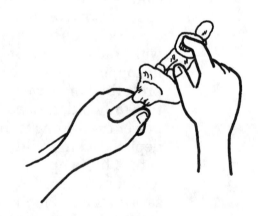

Follow-up

- Have your students make up proverbs or symbolic sayings and illustrate them.

- Hold a parade of linguists with their staffs.

ASIA

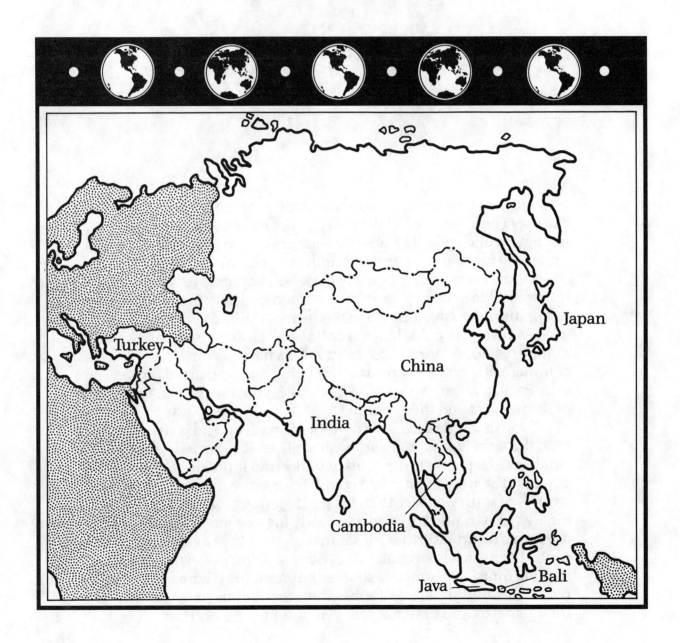

Turkey

Japan

China

India

Cambodia

Java — Bali

Kilims

*T*urkish weaving traditions are firmly rooted in the culture. The kilim is a flat woven rug, meaning that it does not have a thick pile. The weft threads are woven over and under the vertical warp threads and do not loop or stick up.

Kilims are made in a variety of sizes. They are easily transportable and very useful in a nomadic society for wrapping up possessions when on the move. Kilims are also used as covers for cold floors in eating and sitting areas and as mattress foundations. Recently, kilims have become commercially popular and are now being manufactured for sale. Earlier, kilims were made just to meet the everyday needs of the weavers and their families.

Turkish kilims are made of wool from sheep and goats. First the wool is gathered and washed. Then it is carded, or combed, to separate the masses of fibers into individual strands. The wool is spun in a counterclockwise direction. Two strands of spun wool are then twisted together clockwise. Finally, the strands are dyed and ready for weaving. While there are no hard and fast rules for kilim design, many rugs have a central pattern with a contrasting border. Kilim patterns include unusual geometric shapes that combine triangles, rectangles, and squares. Families that wove kilims passed down their patterns and designs from generation to generation.

HOW TO MAKE A
Kilim

Materials

- 1 piece of cardboard, approximately 6 × 8 inches, for each student (Use shirt cardboard or recycle cereal boxes.)
- string or yarn for warp, 10–12 feet

- scissors

- yarn for weaving (the thicker the better)

- other weaving materials (including tinsel, string, pipe cleaners, feathers, fabric scraps, ribbon, straw)

Directions

1. Make a loom by cutting 1-inch notches into the top and bottom corners of the cardboard, 1 inch in from both sides.

2. Knot the warp string close to one end and insert it into the upper left-hand notch.

3. Pull the string down and insert it into the lower left-hand notch. This taut, straight warp string serves as a guide for the other strings.

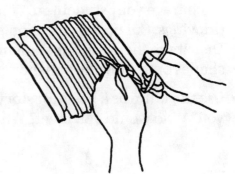

4. Wrap the warp string tightly around both sides of the cardboard, moving from left to right. Leave from $1/2$–1 inch between warp strings.

5. Catch the warp string in the upper right-hand notch and then in the lower right-hand notch. Tie a knot to secure the string in place. When you are done threading your loom, you will have yarn wrapped around both sides of the cardboard. Weave on *one* side only.

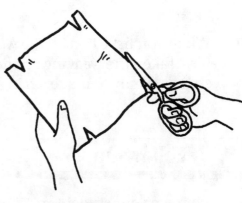

6. Begin weaving by threading weaving material under and over the warp threads. Secure the weaving material by tying it onto the warp threads or by weaving the loose ends in. Some materials will need additional securing with thread or string. Vary the under/over pattern with each row. In other words, if you began the first row weaving under, begin your second row weaving over.

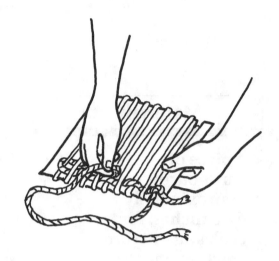

7. Continue weaving to fill up the face of the loom. If you like, make patterns with different stripes, shapes, and textures.

8. When you're finished, turn the loom over so the weaving is face down. Cut the 2 middle warp strings at their center and tie them together twice, at the top and bottom edges of the weaving.

9. Continue cutting and tying off warp strings to the left and right of the 2 middle strings. If you end up with 3 strings, just tie them all together.

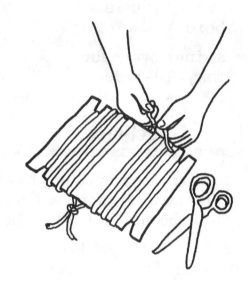

10. When you have tied all the warp strings and have taken the weaving off the loom, cut the strings evenly to make a fringe.

Follow-up

- Encourage your students to create unique geometric shapes by making kilim drawings. Cut up construction paper into small triangles, rectangles, and squares. Distribute them to your students to use in creating new shapes. They can trace the shapes onto drawing paper or graph paper and then color their kilim drawings.

- Use the kilim as a basis for story writing. If your kilim could fly, where would it take you? Who would you meet? What would happen?

Wayang Kulit (Shadow Puppets)

*W*ayang Kulit is the name for Javanese shadow puppets. *Wayang* mean "puppet." *Kulit* means "skin" and refers to the thin buffalo hide the puppets are made of. The wayang are manipulated by the *dhalang,* or puppet master, who also speaks all the voices. The dhalang manipulates the puppets from behind a cotton screen. A light behind the dhalang casts the shadows of the wayang onto the screen. During the performance, a gamelan, a Javanese orchestra of 12 to 40 instruments, plays.

This form of puppet theater is over 1000 years old. Traditionally, the performance is held outdoors or on a porch. It begins at sundown and lasts until the early morning. The stories are long and complicated, filled with many characters and nuances of plot.

The wayang are stylized versions of the Javanese ideal character. The heroes and heroines are slim and small and hold their heads bent in an attitude of humility. Larger puppets look like ogres, symbolizing violent natures and gross habits. They are strong but lack integrity. The ogres are often defeated by the smaller but more righteous heroes and heroines.

HOW TO MAKE A
Wayang Kulit

Materials

- pencils

- tape
- twist ties

- drawing paper or newsprint

- markers

- dowels or sticks: 3 dowels, 16–18 inches long, for each student

- scissors

- paper fasteners

- railroad board or cardboard: 1 piece 7 × 14 inches and 2 pieces 2 × 14

Directions

1. Sketch ideas for figures on drawing paper or newsprint.

2. Cut the drawing into 5 sections. Put the head, body, and legs in 1 section. Divide each arm into 2 sections—shoulder to elbow, and elbow to hand.

3. Place the head, body, and leg section on the 7 × 14-inch piece of railroad board. Place 2 arm sections on each 2 × 14-inch piece. Adjust drawings to fit. Tape and trace with pencil.

4. Cut out the pieces from the railroad board and decorate them with markers.

5. To assemble, place the shoulder of the upper arm section over the shoulder area of the body. Pierce both sections and attach the upper arm to the body with a paper fastener. Repeat to attach the other upper arm.

6. Place the elbow of the lower arm section over the elbow area of the upper arm section.

Pierce both sections and attach the lower arm to the upper arm with a paper fastener. Repeat to attach the other lower arm.

7. Lay a dowel vertically along the center of the puppet body. Mark 4 spots, 2 on each side of the dowel. The pairs of marks should be about 1–2 inches apart vertically.

8. Pierce the marks, and attach the dowel to the puppet body by threading twist ties through the 2 pairs of holes and securing them in the back.

9. Pierce 2 holes in each hand and attach the 2 remaining dowels to the hands using twist ties.

Follow-up

- Stage a puppet play using your entire class and their puppets.

- Have students work in small groups to write an original play that they can perform with their puppets.

- Create a tableau on a bulletin board by arranging the wayang in different positions. Use it as an inspiration for writing or storytelling.

Widyādhari (Guardian Angels)

Life on the Indonesian island of Bali is so infused with art that it is commonly said that all Balinese are artists. People in Bali are exposed to artistic means of expression from early childhood. Their rulers are required to know mythology, history, and poetry, as well as how to paint, carve wood, make musical instruments, sing, and dance. The society includes many painters, carvers, musicians, and dancers. The Balinese expect an artist's work to radiate soulfulness. Artwork is valued more for its emotional power than its technical achievement.

Widyādhari are guardian angels that are suspended over an infant's cradle. Carved out of wood, the winged widyādhari can have the body of a human, animal, bird, dragon, or other imaginary being. The custom of placing widyādhari over an infant's cradle comes from an ancient myth about a family who separated after a baby was born. Images of the baby's mother and father were suspended over the child for strength and protection.

To inspire your students, you may want to share this Balinese quote with them. "Art is thought as expressed by the hands. The essentials are form and life. . . . Peace of mind is necessary for successful work."

HOW TO MAKE A
Widyādhari

Materials

- pencils
- yarn, approximately 1 yard for each student
- scissors
- tag board or railroad board, 1 sheet 11 × 14 inches for each student
- markers

Directions

1. On the tag board, draw an image of a person, an animal, or an imaginary creature that makes you feel good. Be sure to add its outstretched wings.

2. Cut out the widyādhari and color it with markers.

3. Tie one end of the yarn around the neck of the widyādhari and the other end around its back part.

4. Adjust the knots so that the widyādhari hangs evenly when suspended by the yarn. (The body should be horizontal, parallel to the floor and ceiling.)

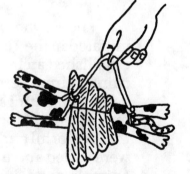

Follow-up

- Hang the widyādhari above the students' seats.

- Ask students to write stories from the widyādhari's perspective. For example, what do they see? How did they come to protect their charges? What do they protect them from?

Miniature Paintings

The Mughal style of Indian miniature painting was initiated in the 16th century by Emperor Akbar, who established an imperial artists' workshop, directed by master painters from Persia. These artists created small, meticulously detailed paintings, which were bound into albums and manuscripts. Mughal emperors dictated the subject matter of these colorful and luminous paintings. Therefore, the images were varied and included epic stories, court scenes, portraits, animals, and flowers.

To make the paintings, artists applied opaque watercolors to paper. They achieved fine detailing with the aid of tiny brushes. They then surrounded the pictures with carefully rendered borders, which were frequently painted in a metallic color. Sometimes the artists incorporated writing into the images. The dimensions of these miniature paintings ranged from 7 × 14 inches to 10 × 14 inches.

HOW TO MAKE A
Miniature Painting

Materials

- scrap paper
- watercolor brushes
- watercolors or gouache
- metallic crayons (optional)

- pencils
- water
- paper (drawing or watercolor), approximately 4 × 5½ inches

- erasers
- containers for water
- newspaper to cover tables

Directions

1. Think of a person, place, or animal. It can be real or imaginary. Sketch your idea onto the scrap paper or the paper you will paint on. Leave room around the edges for a decorative border.

2. After the central image has been drawn, create the border by repeating geometric shapes or images related to your subject matter.

3. Paint the image with watercolor. Let dry.

4. Use metallic watercolor or metallic crayons to highlight the image and the border.

- Have your students write a story or a poem about their miniature painting. Mount the story or poem and the painting on a larger piece of paper. Bind everyone's work into a book or album for the class to enjoy all year long.

- Invite each student to write a simple story. Divide the class into pairs. Have each partner read the other partner's story and create a miniature painting to illustrate a key scene. Share everyone's work with the class.

- Give each student a sheet of paper. Have students fold (then unfold) the paper so that they each have 8 "boxes" of the same size. Ask students to think of a simple story they can communicate in 8 tiny pictures (but no words). Then have them draw a sketch in each box. Finally, encourage students to share their "picture stories" with classmates.

- Take this opportunity to think about the word *miniature*. Discuss the word's meaning. Does *miniature* mean the same as *small?* Why or why not? Brainstorm a list of other things that are miniature. If you like, encourage students to bring in miniature items for a "teeny-tiny show and tell."

Woodblock Prints

*P*rint making is a vital art form worldwide. Japanese print making dates back to A.D. 770. Early prints were black line drawings, carved from cherry wood blocks and printed on white paper. Eventually, colors were added by hand. During the sixteenth century, printed book illustrations became very popular, and a method of applying color within the printing process was developed. At the same time, Japan's wealthy population offered lavish commissions to the makers of beautiful calendars. Artists and craftspeople collaborated to refine a Chinese technique that allowed them to print multiple colors on one image with great accuracy.

The high point of Japanese woodblock printing was during the Kansei era, 1789–1801. Images with as many as 18 different colors described aspects of daily life, views of nature, and themes from poetry. Artists, printers, carvers, and publishers worked within a strict hierarchy to produce prints. Publishers frequently made the most money, and artists were often very poor. Black-ink printers, the lowest of the printers, were called "drainage ditch printers" or "guttersnipes." In contemporary Japan, artists design and make their own prints, operating independently from the older hierarchy.

Japanese artists frequently organize their images around specific themes. For example, the color print maker Hokusai (1760–1849) did a series of prints called "Thirty-six Views of Mt. Fuji." Mt. Fuji appears in each print, sometimes as the dominant and obvious center of attention, sometimes relegated to the background. You may want to suggest that your students organize their images around a theme or topic. Each student has an opportunity to describe a unique perspective.

HOW TO MAKE A
Print

Materials

- water-soluble markers
- scissors
- water-soluble printing ink
- sticks or ball-point pens
- masking tape
- smooth plastic foam trays (recycled from the grocery store or ordered from a craft store)
- small sponges
- brayers
- rice paper or drawing paper, cut a few inches larger than the plastic foam trays

HOW TO MAKE A
Printing Plate or Block

Directions

1. Cut the curved edges off a plastic foam tray to obtain a flat rectangular surface. One side should be completely smooth.

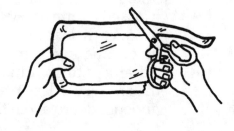

2. Using water-soluble markers, sketch an idea for a print onto the smooth side of the plastic tray. Be sure to press very lightly. Use small sponges moistened with water to erase any mistakes.

3. When your drawing is completed, use a stick or ball-point pen to press firmly into the plastic foam, "carving" your design. Reinforce the back of the tray with masking tape if it weakens. After you have carved your design, you are ready to print.

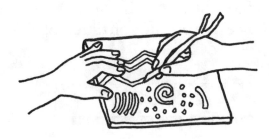

HOW TO
Print

It's a good idea to roll up (that is, apply ink to the plates) in one area and print in another. Rolling up can be messy! You may want to use two separate tables for rolling up and printing.

Directions

1. Squeeze out a small amount of water-soluble printing ink onto a medium-size plastic foam tray (with its curved edges intact). Roll out the ink with a brayer.

2. Roll the inked brayer onto the carved plate. Apply enough ink to cover the uncarved areas evenly. Move the plate to the printing area.

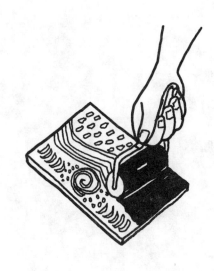

3. Place rice paper or drawing paper on top of the inked plate. Rub the entire surface firmly and evenly with your hands. (One advantage of rice paper is that its translucency makes it easy to see the ink transfer from the plate to the paper.)

4. Carefully peel the paper off the inked plate. Sign your print with a pencil and hang it up to dry.

5. Also wash your plates if you want to print from them again. Wash your brayers.

If possible, let each student print more than once. Try printing on different types of paper.

Follow-up

- Have students mount their prints on construction paper, then decorate the borders with different colors of paper. Display the works in your classroom.

- Ask each student to title his or her print. Laminate the prints and bind them together to create a class book to share with parents during Open House.

- Invite students to write a haiku, a Japanese poem of 17 syllables whose subject is usually something in nature that has moved the poet.

- Ask students to trade prints with classmates. Then have each student use their classmate's print as a springboard to writing by asking: "How does the image make you feel? Write a paragraph describing that feeling."

Scrolls

China has an ancient history of writing. As early as in
1500 B.C. the Chinese wrote on bones and tortoise shells. Later
they used lacquered boards and bamboo as writing surfaces
and still later, silk. In A.D. 105, a Chinese government employee,
Ts'ai Lun, was frustrated with his choices of writing surfaces.
Wood was too heavy and silk was too expensive. So he
combined tree bark, plant fibers, hemp, old rags, and fishing
nets and came up with—paper.

The key ingredient in paper is cellulose, which is found in
cotton, linen, and other plant fibers. Cellulose makes tiny
threadlike structures that bond together to form paper. A writing
surface that is *not* made of cellulose is not paper. For example,
parchment and vellum are not paper.

Scrolls made from papyrus, parchment, paper, and fabric
have been used by people all over the world. In China, hanging
scrolls are displayed vertically. Longer scrolls are displayed
horizontally and unrolled gradually for viewing in sections. It is
quite possible that pagination was developed as a method of
finding one's place in a very long scroll.

The paper used in this project is called rice paper, but it is
not made of rice. It is made from the inner white bark of several
varieties of young Japanese trees and different grasses. Very
thin, yet strong, it is made in Japan.

One theme of this project is sequence. Your students can tell a story, write or copy a poem, or describe changes in nature. They can make an autobiographical scroll in which they describe something they remember from their past, something they are doing in the present, and any hopes or dreams they have for the future.

HOW TO MAKE A
Scroll

Materials

- 2 dowels or sticks, 14 inches
- ribbon or string
- water-soluble markers
- fine-line indelible markers

- rulers
- watercolors
- glue sticks
- rice paper or drawing paper, 9 × 24 inches

- masking tape
- brushes
- pencils
- newsprint or drawing paper, 9 × 24-inch sheets

Directions

1. Hold the newsprint or drawing paper horizontally. Rule off 1-inch margins on the left and right edges of the paper. Make a 2-inch margin on the lower edge.

2. Sketch your idea within the margins. Create a simple drawing with strong outlines.

3. Place the rice paper over the newsprint sketch and tape it along the edges. Check to make sure you can see the original drawing. Make any changes, additions, or corrections on the original.

4. Using the indelible markers, trace lightly over the drawing. Remain within the margins. Indicate textures and details. Keep the papers taped together.

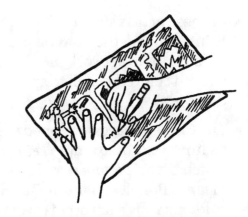

5. Paint over the outline using different watercolor techniques: wet on wet, dry brush, and regular wash. (You can tell students that brush strokes are the fingerprints of a painting. They can use different types of brush strokes to emphasize the uniqueness of their work.) Expect the paint to spread, or bleed, on this type of paper. Let dry and untape the rice paper carefully.

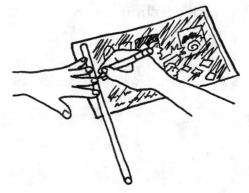

6. Write a description of the sequence of images in the drawing in the bottom margin. It can be a story, poem, or dialogue.

7. Lay a dowel down on the rice paper to determine where to apply glue.

8. Mark with pencil and apply glue.

9. Place the dowel on the rice paper. Press and roll, adhering paper all around the dowel.

10. Repeat to attach a dowel to the other side. Let dry.

11. Color dowels with water-soluble markers.

12. Roll up the scroll and tie it with ribbon or string.

Follow-up

- Divide the class into groups of 2–5 to unroll and read their scrolls to each other.

- Have a scroll reading party. Give each student an opportunity to stand in front of the class to display and read his or her scroll. Encourage students to ask questions about one another's scrolls.

- Chinese artists sign their work with chops, or seals, that record a name or phrase. Printed in red, they can be square, round, or oval. Frequently other people add their chops to artwork they look at. Have your students develop chops. They can use red colored pencil to apply them to their own scrolls and to other scrolls they view.

- The Chinese have developed specific terminologies for different painting techniques. For example *Fei-pei* means "Flying white" and refers to a technique in which paint is applied so that streaks of white paper show through. *Mei-kuhua* means "Boneless painting" and refers to a painting without any outlines. As your students view each other's work, have them make up their own names for the painting techniques.

- Chinese scrolls make wonderful presents. Encourage students to give them to grandparents, parents, siblings, or friends. (They might want to create scrolls with stories to honor these special people.)

Hmong Story Cloths

*T*he Hmong people are originally from southern China, Burma, and Laos. Because they were nomadic and frequently on the move, their material culture was of necessity light and easily transportable. Traditional Hmong costumes called *paj mtaub* or "flower cloth" are incredibly complex and beautiful combinations of appliqué, reverse appliqué, embroidery, and batik. Traditionally, girls learned these techniques at an early age. Uses of contemporary Hmong flower cloth have expanded beyond the making of traditional costumes to encompass a variety of textile objects. Men now take an active part in the manufacture and sale of these textiles.

Hmong story cloths are banners that use some of the traditional techniques. They are like pictures or paintings made from different types of fabrics that are sewn together. The story cloths describe aspects of Hmong life, including a well-known legend about a woman who fends off the tiger that killed her husband and wants to take his place. Another shows a legendary giant flood that divided the Hmong into families or clans. Other story cloths portray life in a Hmong village or in America. Many Hmong story cloths made in America today intentially incorporate written English into their composition in order to teach English.

HOW TO MAKE A
Story Cloth

Materials

- drawing paper or newsprint, 12 × 14 inches
- tape
- fabric scraps (use felt for easier cutting)

- pencils
- markers
- fabric panels, approximately 12 × 14 inches

- scissors
- fabric glue
- needles, thread, embroidery thread (optional)

Directions

1. Sketch ideas for the depiction of a favorite story or image on the drawing paper.

2. Cut out the most important shapes from the sketch.

3. Tape the paper shapes onto fabric scraps and trace them with a marker.

4. Cut out fabric shapes and arrange them on the fabric panel.

5. Tape the shapes in place, then glue or sew them onto the panel.

6. Write words on the story cloth with pencil or marker.

7. Sew over the letters with embroidery thread if you like.

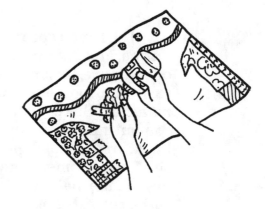

Follow-up

- Share by having each student hold up his or her story cloth and describe it to the class.

- Have students (temporarily) trade story cloths with classmates. Ask each student to look at his or her classmate's story cloth and use it as a springboard for a story. To get students in the frame of mind for writing, ask questions such as: "What do you think your classmate was trying to say in his or her cloth? What does that remind you of? Write a story about it."

- To display, sew or glue all the story cloths together to make a story cloth quilt.

- Invite other classes over to view your story cloth quilt. Encourage them to create their own story cloth quilts and invite *you* over!

EUROPE

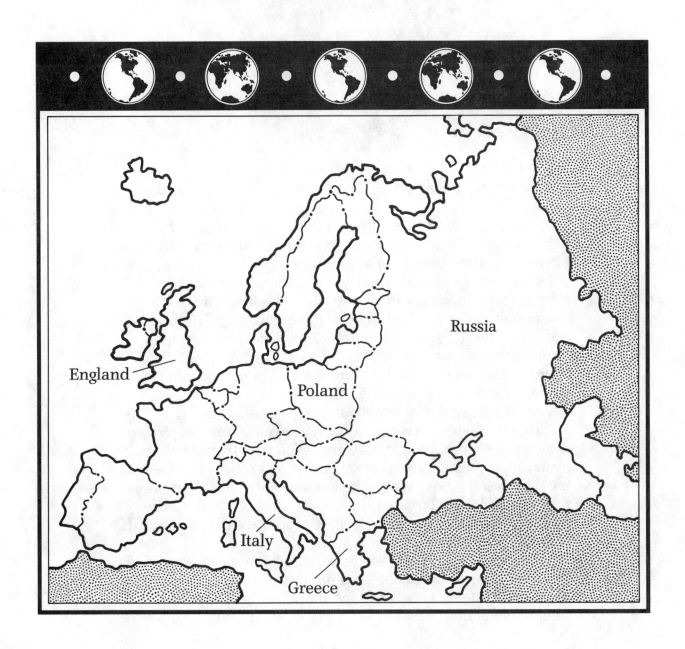

England

Russia

Poland

Italy

Greece

Rocking Horses

Rocking horses are popular children's toys all over the world. They evolved from horses on sticks and miniature horses on wheels. The development of rocking horses in England parallels the changes in the role of the horse and links British affection for the horse with a traditional love of children.

Horses in England were originally important for their strength and durability in farming and in battle. Mid-seventeenth-century-England saw the importing of Arabian stallions. Standing taller than their European counterparts, these horses were strong and fast. Simultaneously, the countryside was changing. Woodland and marsh became pasture. Common land was fenced in. The landed gentry developed the sports of hedge jumping and fox hunting.

In the nineteenth century, the horse population exploded as steam power and railroads were developed. Increased wealth promoted equestrian recreation, and the number of equestrian toys increased. The first rocking horses in England were horse shapes attached to large semicircular pieces of wood. As the craft developed, the rockers became separate sculptural motifs, graceful and sinuous curves.

Rocking horses are made out of pine planks that are glued together. Craftspeople carve and paint the wood, then screw the horses onto the rockers. The eyes, mane, and tail are the finishing touches.

HOW TO MAKE A

Rocking Horse

Materials

- drawing paper or newsprint, 11 × 10 inches

- railroad board or tag board, 11 × 14 inches

- pencils

- tape

- scissors

- markers

Directions

1. To make a pattern, first position the drawing paper so that the 11-inch sides form the bottom and top. Sketch a horse in action. Draw 1 arch connecting the legs to make a rocker.

2. Cut out the pattern of the horse and rocker. Cut off the head at the base of the neck, making a line even with the horse's back. (Don't worry, this is a temporary situation.)

3. Fold a sheet of railroad board in half so it looks like 2 pieces of 11 × 7-inch board.

4. Place the pattern of the horse's body and rocker on the folded board so that the horse's back lies along the fold. Tape the pattern to the board and trace it.

5. Cut out the horse and rocker that you traced, but leave this side connected along the fold to the uncut, untraced side. For a sturdier rocking horse, do *not* cut out the section between the horse's belly, legs, and rocker.

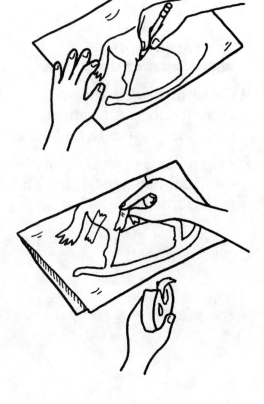

6. Using the cutout side as a pattern, trace the horse and rocker onto the uncut side of the railroad board.

7. Cut out the second side.

8. Tape the pattern for the head to a leftover scrap of railroad board. Trace, the pattern adding a $1/2$-inch tab to the bottom of the neck.

9. Cut out the head and make a small horizontal cut (approximately $1/2$–1 inch) in the tab at the base of the neck. This will act as a notch, to keep the head in place when it is joined to the body.

10. Make a small cut along the fold where the base of the neck and the body connect.

11. Place the head inside the cut, using the notch to hold it in place along the fold.

12. Color the rocking horse with markers.

Follow-up

• Create an English rocking horse museum by displaying the rocking horses with written information about the creation of each piece. Your students can include their name, the date, and the materials they used.

• Ask students to write a story from the perspective of the rocking horse. They may want to think about who the horse's favorite rider is, where the horse would like to go, its favorite music for rocking, and so on.

Marionettes

Marionettes, hinged puppets suspended and manipulated by a series of strings, are known the world over. They have been found in Egyptian tombs as well as in Greek excavations. Bil Baird, a well-known contemporary puppeteer, thinks they evolved from the hinged mask. The origin of the name marionette is uncertain. Some people think the puppets were brought to France during the reign of Charles IX (1560–74) by an Italian named Marion.

The popular puppets Punch and Judy, were originally English versions of characters in a marionette play by the Italian puppeteer Puccini. Pinocchio, another well-known marionette celebrated his hundredth birthday in 1981. A Florentine author, Carlo Collodi, was unable to pay a small gambling debt. Instead, he agreed to write a serialized story for a children's magazine and Pinocchio was born.

A popular Italian marionette drama of the late 1600s, *Orlando Furioso* was a fantasy about Roland, the eighth-century knight and nephew of Charlemagne. Productions of *Orlando Furioso* included 300 characters, among them, foot soldiers, witches, dragons, angels, and devils. The wooden puppets were between four and five feet tall. With armor, some puppets weighed as much as 80 pounds.

This is a difficult project that you may want to do with older students. Making marionettes involves some knowledge of the parts of the human body and the way they fit together. You can familiarize your students with anatomy by looking at each other and at pictures of human skeletons and by identifying different joints, body parts, and connections.

HOW TO MAKE A
Marionette

Materials

- **wire cutters**
- **fabric strips**
- **feathers**
- **armature wire, approximately 6 feet for each student: two 10-inch pieces (body), one 7-inch piece (head and neck), two 8-inch pieces (arms), two 9-inch pieces (legs)**

- **newspaper**
- **fabric scraps**
- **buttons**
- **yarn or string: one 10-inch piece, one 12-inch piece, two 14-inch pieces, two 17-inch pieces**

- **masking tape**
- **scissors**
- **fabric glue**

Directions

1. To form the body, take the two 10-inch pieces of wire and twist them together to make an ⊥ shape. The vertical section should be about 3 inches long. The top and bottom horizontal sections should be quite long— about 3 inches each.

2. To form the shoulder and hip sockets, bend the ends of the horizontal wires back to the center, making loops.

3. To form the neck and head, attach the 7-inch wire to the "spinal column," or the vertical part of the ⊥ shape.

4. Bend this wire to make a head shape (profile or full view), and twist any extra wire around the neck.

5. To form the arms, attach one 8-inch piece of wire to each shoulder socket loop. Bend the end of the arm wire into a loop and twist any extra wire back around the arm. Loops should be open enough to allow for movement. (It may be helpful to form the loops by first wrapping the wire around a pencil.)

6. Bend the loose ends of the arm wires to make hand shapes.

7. To form the legs and feet, use the 9-inch wires and follow the same procedure to attach the legs to the hip sockets.

8. To make knee and elbow joints, cut arm and leg wires at the midpoints. Make open loops to connect upper-arm to lower-arm wires and upper-leg to lower-leg wires. (This step is optional.)

9. Add muscle and flesh to the bones by crumpling up newspaper and wrapping it around the wires. Use masking tape to keep it in place. Be sure to leave all the joints open to allow for mobility.

10. Cover newspaper-wrapped bodies, head, arms, and legs with fabric strips. Tape 1 end of a fabric strip to the body and tightly wrap the fabric around the body, overlapping edges of the fabric so that the newspaper does not show through. Tape, glue, or tuck under the ends of the fabric to avoid unraveling.

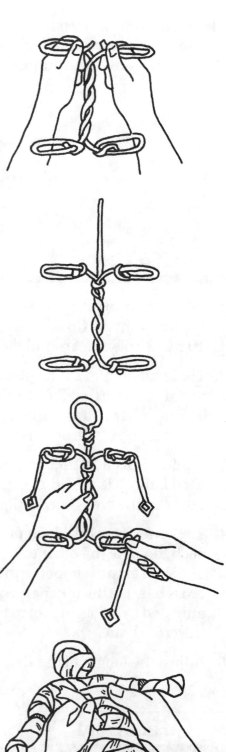

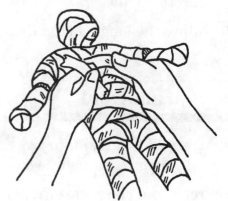

11. Make costumes using fabric scraps, feathers, and buttons. Assemble the costumes and attach them to the puppet with fabric glue.

HOW TO ASSEMBLE THE
Marionette

Directions

1. Make the control by crossing the 2 dowels to form a + shape. Crisscross approximately 10 inches of yarn around the intersection to secure.

2. Tie 1 end of the 12-inch piece of yarn to the top of the wire that forms the puppet's head. Tie the other end to the control at the intersection of the dowels.

3. Tie 1 end of each 14-inch piece of yarn onto each hand. Tie the other ends next to each other on the cross bar section of the control.

4. Tie 1 end of each 17-inch piece of yarn onto each foot. Tie the other end of the yarn attached to the left foot to the left side of the cross bar. Tie the other end of the yarn attached to the right foot to the right side of the cross bar.

5. Adjust the length of the strings if necessary.

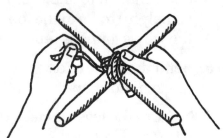

Follow-up

- Arrange for students to practice manipulating their marionettes. Have them try to make their marionettes walk, jump, skip, and dance.

- Break your class into groups and organize puppet plays, or have your entire class create and perform a puppet play.

Wycinanki (Paper Cutouts)

$\mathcal{P}$aper cutouts were a simple, practical way for rural Polish people to decorate the interiors of their buildings. Derived from the older traditions of leather and cloth cutouts, paper cutouts were made by folding glossy paper along one or two axes and then cutting it with sheep shears. By carefully manipulating the placement and shape of the cuts, it was possible to create intricate designs and even scenes. Daily life, religious events, and technical innovations have all appeared in wycinanki.

Traditionally, the Poles made the paper cutouts in the fall and spring. Wycinanki have been found in rural cottages and in libraries and other public buildings.

Learning about symmetry and symmetrical relationships is an inherent aspect of this project. One way of introducing symmetry, or the concept of balance occurring along an axis, is to look at things that are naturally symmetrical—faces and butterflies, for example. You can also have your students look at things that are not symmetrical and discuss why. Students can then create symmetrical compositions using shapes of familiar objects or of things they have created.

HOW TO MAKE A
Wycinanki

Materials

- **scrap paper**
- **colored construction paper, $8^{1}/_{2} \times 11$ inches or larger**
- **scissors**
- **pencils**

Directions

1. Practice paper cutting first. Fold scrap paper in half and cut a few simple shapes into the paper, starting from the folded edge. Open up the paper to see what the cutouts look like. Continue practicing if you like.

2. Think of a simple design using geometric shapes, animals, people, plants, or imaginary creatures. You may want to sketch the shapes on scrap paper and use them as patterns to trace.

3. Fold construction paper in half or along the axis you need to use to carry out your idea.

4. Draw shapes onto the folded construction paper. If you are using a pattern, trace just *half* of the shape.

5. Cut along the lines you have drawn, or experiment and just cut shapes you like. (Let your scissors talk!)

6. Repeat folding, drawing, and cutting to add shapes or refine your idea.

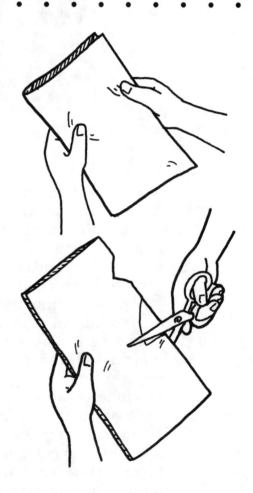

7. Open up the paper and change the shape of the outer edges by cutting additional shapes or patterns.

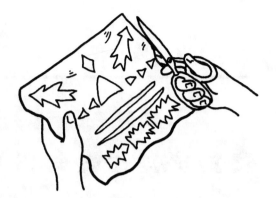

Follow-up

- Have students mount their wycinanki on slightly larger pieces of contrasting color paper. Display them in your classroom or school.

- Divide the class into groups to share their wycinanki and to discuss how they came up with different shapes, designs, and compositions.

- Laminate and bind together your students' artworks to form a class book. Share the book with parents during Open House.

- Have students (temporarily) exchange their wycinanki with classmates. Encourage students to use that artwork as a springboard to writing by asking questions such as: "How does the wycinanki make you feel? What does it look like? What does it remind you of? Write about it."

Flax Dolls

World-wide, dolls are created as an impetus for imaginative play. Doll making is a popular Russian craft. People in the countryside made dolls during the winter to earn extra money. In the agriculatural regions of central Russia, children tied small straw dolls to their necks, wrists, and waists. In the forest regions and northern Russia, people made dolls out of pine cones, birch bark, and dried moss. In western Russia, advanced plaiting techniques were utilized to create dolls out of flax and straw. Flax dolls wore a variety of costumes and were engaged in many activities, from playing the accordion or the guitar to holding babies or farming tools.

HOW TO MAKE A
Flax Doll

Materials

- **straw, twigs, pine needles, or yarn**
- **scissors**
- **yarn, thread, or pipe cleaners**
- **glue**

1. To form the head, body, and legs, gather together a bundle of like-size pieces of straw or other material. The bundle should be at least 1 inch thick.

2. Tie the bundle together at the neck by wrapping it with yarn, thread, or a pipe cleaner.

3. The part below the neck serves as the body and the legs. Separate the lower section into 2 legs. Wrap and tie yarn, at the ankles. (Add more straw to the legs if you need to.)

4. Gather another bundle of straw to use for the arms. Attach it to the body at the chest by criss-crossing and then tying yarn around the arm bundle and the body.

5. Make hands by wrapping and tying yarn at the wrists.

6. Add facial features by gluing yarn pieces onto the head.

7. Use pipe cleaners and yarn to add any costume elements (belts, hats, etc.) or to make tools (rakes, canes, etc.).

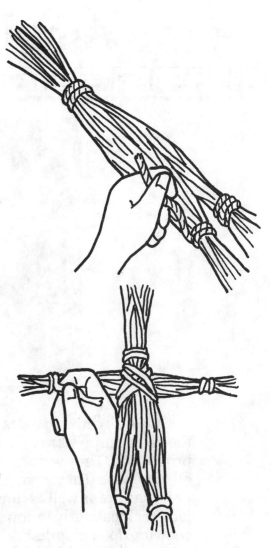

Follow-up

- Display by tacking the dolls onto a bulletin board in your classroom or school. Have your students write descriptive pieces about their dolls.

- Use the dolls as an impetus for writing dialogue. Break up your class into small groups. Let the students use their dolls to initiate conversations that they record in writing or on tape.

Amphorae (Urns)

Greek ceramic vases created between the eleventh and the sixth centuries B.C. are renowned for their beauty and proportion. They were used to store and transport olives, cereal, oil, and wine. They were painted with designs and scenes from everyday life as well as illustrations of poems and myths. In fact, such painterly innovations as expressing emotion by showing open mouths and other facial expressions were initiated on the sides of these ceramic vases.

The vases or urns are more correctly referred to as amphorae (amphora is the singular). Amphorae are narrow at the bottom and often have a foot or small platform or disk as a base. They are broad at the shoulders and have a narrower neck. Two handles are attached to the widest part. The average height of an amphora is 18 inches, but they range from 12 inches to five feet tall. The smallest amphorae are called amphoriskoi.

To make amphorae, Greek potters first washed their clay to rid it of any unwanted stones. Then they wedged the clay to remove pockets of air. Amphorae were made on a potter's wheel. The potter placed the clay in the middle of the wheel, centered it, and pulled it up into its finished form in a process called throwing a pot. Then the handles were attached and the amphora was polished and glazed. The last step was firing in a kiln.

Potters' implements from classical Greece have not survived but images of the ceramic studio have. Some amphorae paintings depict potters working at the wheel, measuring tools, and kilns.

You might like to share this quote with your students before beginning the amphora project. "Potters turn the wheel which moves neither backward nor forward and at the same time imitates the rotation of the universe, and on the same wheel as it whirls they make things of all kinds, no one of them like another, from the same materials with the same tools."

HOW TO MAKE AN
Amphora

Materials

- clay, 2 balls, 3–4 inches in diameter, for each student

- water

- red, white, and black tempera paint

- brushes

- clay tools—old pencils, old toothbrushes, sticks, etc.

Directions

1. Take 1 of the balls of clay and roll it between your palms or on the table to make it really round.

2. Hold the ball of clay in your palm. Press the thumb from your other hand into the center of the clay. Stop before you go all the way through!

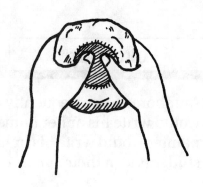

3. With your thumb inside the ball of clay, place your fingers on the outside. Press your fingers and thumb toward each other, and release.

4. Turn the clay slowly and repeat. Continue turning and pressing until you have created a bowl-like form. Use a little water to smooth out any cracks that may develop.

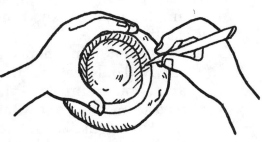

5. Make coils, or snake shapes, out of the second ball of clay by breaking off pieces and rolling them out on the table.

6. Add coils to the bottom of the bowl form to make a base and to the top to make a neck. Score, or texture, the bowl with a clay tool where you plan to add the coils. Be sure to texture the coil section as well. Add a touch of water to help join the pieces and smooth them together.

7. Roll out 2 coils for handles. Make sure they are not too thin.

8. Texture the coils and the bowl where they will be attached. Moisten with water, attach, and smooth. Let dry.

9. If you have access to a kiln, fire your amphora. If not, handle it carefully.

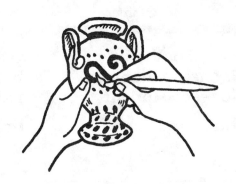

10. Decorate your amphora using black, red, and white tempera paint. You can paint designs, scenes from everyday life, athletic events, or depictions of myths or poems. Let dry.

Follow-up

- Amphorae were frequently inscribed with the names of their creators. The potter would write his or her name and then *epoiesen,* which translates as "made." The painter would write his or her name and then *egrapsen,* "painted." Have your students sign their names to their work in this manner.

- Make a mini-museum in which to display the amphorae. To accompany their amphorae, have students write short descriptions about what they intend each amphora to be used for.

- Use the amphorae as a springboard to writing by reading students this story starter: *I walked into the living room and couldn't believe my eyes! I picked up my amphora and inside I saw a . . .*

- Have your students write poems about their amphorae. They can write about what the amphorae hold and who uses them, the illustration on the exterior, or life from the amphora's point of view.

- Amphorae make wonderful presents. Encourage students to give their amphorae to a mother, father, grandparent, or special friend.

- Research wildflowers that are indigenous to your region. Pick those wildflowers and display them in your students' amphorae.

AUSTRALIA

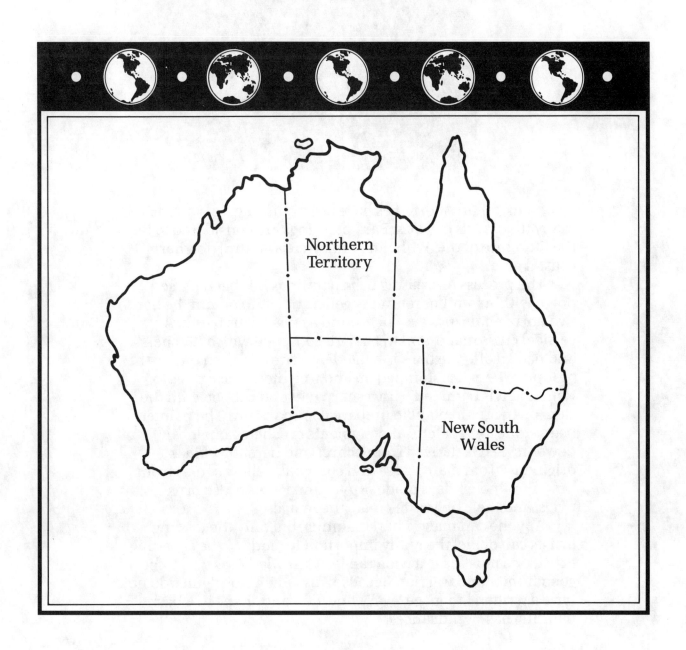

Northern
Territory

New South
Wales

Aboriginal Bark Paintings

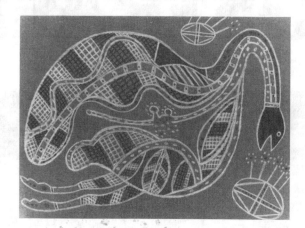

*A*ustralian Aborigines have been painting on bark for many thousands of years. Bark paintings are considered to be the literature of the Arnheim Land Area, a central northern coastal area.

The process of creating bark paintings has been passed down within families for many generations. To obtain the bark, two horizontal rings are cut around a eucalyptus trunk. A vertical cut is made, and the bark is loosened with a hatchet and peeled off. The bark is heated by a fire and then put on the ground, where it is stomped on and weighted with stones to flatten it. It is trimmed with a sharp tool and rubbed with the stem of an orchid plant to prepare it for painting. The painters use a stone for a palette and pigments crushed from local powders. Red is derived from ochres and hematite, black originates from manganese and charcoal, yellow comes from limonite, and white is made of gypsum. Painters use brushes, twigs, and their fingers to create the images.

Anyone can make a bark painting, but only the leading artists can depict the really important legends. To be a leading artist, one must have a wide range of knowledge as well as be a good hunter and warrior. Because Australian Aborigines do not have a written language, every line, dot, and shape in a bark painting has significance.

Many bark paintings show a kind of X-ray vision. They depict the inner organs and skeletons of animals and humans. This X-ray style, sometimes called *skeletonization,* has been unchanged for 10,000 years and may be one of the oldest painting traditions in the world.

HOW TO MAKE AN
Aboriginal Bark Painting

Materials

- **brown, tan, or ochre construction paper or recycled brown paper bags**

- **colored pencils: brown, black, yellow, white, red**

- **erasers**

Directions

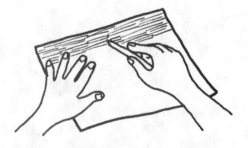

1. Using the side of a brown or black pencil, rub over the entire surface of the paper to create a texture and give a barklike feeling.

2. Draw the outline of a person or animal. (Don't forget kangaroos and dingoes!)

3. Show some of the bones and internal organs. (This drawing does not have to be anatomically correct but should give the basic idea.)

4. Fill in the open spaces with other figures and patterns of dots, crosshatching, stripes, and other designs.

Follow-up

- According to standards of Australian Aboriginal aesthetics, a painting is not considered a work of art unless its meaning is understood. Beauty is related to how much the viewer's imagination is stimulated. Working in small groups, children can free associate about each member's painting. A spokesperson can report back to the class with the group's responses.

- As a class, explore the trees in your community. What is the bark like? Do you think any would be appropriate to paint or draw on? Why or why not? (Those of you who live near birch trees are in luck!)

- Use the pictures as a springboard to writing. Invite students to write a story about the person or animal in their bark painting. Encourage students to share their stories with the class.

Aboriginal Dream Maps

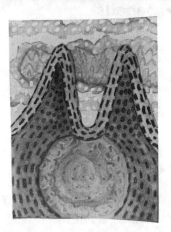

*A*ustralian Aborigines have been recording their dreamings, or ancestral mythologies, for many generations. In the 1930s, anthropologists gave Australian Aborigines brown paper and crayons and asked them to draw whatever they wanted. The native Australians drew maps and landscapes of mythological events. The Aborigines believe that every place has a story.

In the 1970s, Australian Aborigines began painting their dream maps using acrylic paint on canvas. The compositions are usually symmetrical and composed of arcs, circles, ovals, straight and curved lines, and many, many dots. Frequently, paintings are group efforts. A *kirda,* or the most knowledgeable person, sketches out the main aspects of the composition. Then a more experienced painter takes over and finishes the work. Sometimes people help each other paint the multitude of dots.

Australian Aborigines have names for their dot patterns and designs. Share these with your students for inspiration:

::::::::: **yirarni kanardi = walking straight**

 rdaku karirdakukar = to go from hole to hole

wirlki wirlki yirrarni = clusters of boomerangs

HOW TO MAKE AN
Aboriginal Dream Map

Materials

- white drawing paper, 8½ × 11 inches or larger
- watercolors
- pencils
- brushes
- craypas or crayons

Directions

1. Sketch an idea for a landscape on the drawing paper. It can be an imaginary scene, a real place, or a dream image.

2. Use craypas or crayons to apply color and accentuate special parts of your drawing. Be sure to leave some white paper showing.

3. Apply watercolors to the drawing. Because watercolor resists oil and grease, it will not stick to the crayoned area but will adhere to the blank paper instead. Let dry.

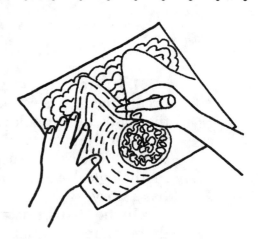

Follow-up

- Have students mount their dream maps on construction paper to display in your room.

- Have each student pick another child's dream map and write a story about it.

- Divide your class into groups and have them come up with ideas for group dream maps that they can then draw and paint.

GREENLAND

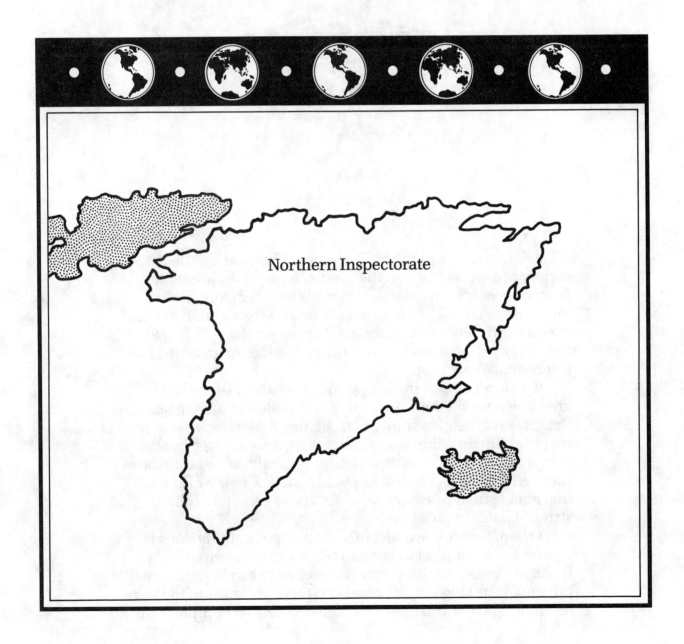

Northern Inspectorate

Eskimo Dolls

*D*olls that are made by Eskimos in Greenland reflect a variety of aspects of life in the tundra. Many dolls are made from bone, hide, and sinew, materials left over from hunted land game and sea mammals. Eskimos have great skill as bone carvers and frequently make doll bodies and faces from carved bone. They wrap the dolls with fur and sealskin, imitating the traditional Arctic costume.

The Inuit, one of the indigenous peoples of Greenland, are known for their inventiveness and skilled craftsmanship. Examples of their ingenuity in designing tools from available materials include the oil lamp, dog sled, *umiak* (large boat), skin tent, and kayak. Eskimo dolls frequently carry accessories such as hunting tackle and kayaks, models of real-world tools that enable their northern creators to succeed in their hard struggle for existence.

One of the truly wonderful things about making dolls is that even the simplest forms can represent the human body. If you are working with young children, you can simplify this project by making just the head and torso (leaving out the steps for making arms and legs) and then dressing the simple form.

HOW TO MAKE AN
Eskimo Doll

Materials

- newspaper
- fabric glue
- scissors
- yarn
- pencils
- sticks or twigs
- synthetic fur scraps
- construction paper

Directions

1. Crumple 1–2 sheets of newspaper to create a cylindrical shape for the head and body.

2. Tie a piece of yarn around the neck to create the head and body and hold the newspaper together.

3. Crumple another sheet of newspaper. This piece should be longer and thinner since it will be used to create the arms.

4. Attach the arms to the body just below the neck by crisscrossing yarn over the arms and body and then tying it.

5. Tie a piece of yarn at each wrist, to form arms, wrists, and hands.

6. Crumple another sheet of newspaper for the legs. It should be about the same size as the piece for the arms.

7. Fold the newspaper for the legs in half, and tie it onto the body at the waist.

8. Tie a piece of yarn at each ankle to make the legs, ankles, and feet.

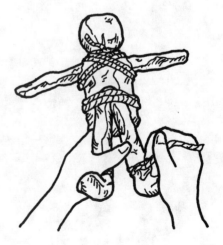

9. Use synthetic fur scraps to clothe the dolls in jackets, pants, boots, mittens, and hoods. Attach the clothes by tying them on with yarn or by gluing them on.

10. Draw a face and features on construction paper. Cut it out and glue it onto the newspaper head.

11. Use sticks, twigs, and leftover materials to fashion tools and accessories.

Follow-up

- Display students' Eskimo dolls on a bulletin board along with poems and stories about what students imagine Arctic life is like in Greenland.

- Divide your class into groups, and have your students role-play scenes of family life, using their dolls.